Library of
Davidson College

Futurism
AND FUTURE STUDIES
by Draper L. Kauffman, Jr.

Second Edition

nea
National Education Association
Washington, D.C.

370.1
K21f

Acknowledgments
The manuscript of this book has been reviewed by Deane C. Thompson, social studies teacher, Willowbrook High School, Villa Park, Illinois.

Copyright © 1976, 1980
National Education Association of the United States
Stock No. 1803-6-00

Library of Congress Cataloging in Publication Data

Kauffman, Draper L. 1946–
    Futurism and future studies.

    (Developments in classroom instruction)
    Bibliography: p.
    1. Education—Philosophy. 2. Forecasting. 3. Educational planning. I. Title. II. Series.
LB885.K3414   371.2'07   75-35589
ISBN 0-8106-1803-6

81-9379

CONTENTS

	Author's Preface to the Second Edition	5
1.	Introduction	7
2.	The Alternative Futures Approach	11
3.	Systems, Stability, and Change	17
4.	Key Issues	29
5.	The Psychology of the Future	43
	References	49
	Bibliography	55

The Author

Draper L. Kauffman, Jr., is the president of D & D Associates, St. Louis, Missouri. Dr. Kauffman previously conducted Future Studies courses at Webster College and at the University of Massachusetts. Among his publications are *Teaching the Future* and *The Human Environment*.

Author's Preface to the Second Edition

A second printing of this monograph means, to me, that it has been of some value to people and the publishers think it will endure, at least for a while longer.

Still, there was a sense of trepidation, as well, when I went back to reread. Would I, the toughest critic to please, still be happy with it? This is particularly a problem when writing about the future of *anything* in this turbulent age. Such books often age badly. How well has this one held up?

Conveniently for the author, but unfortunately for most readers, there is little in the first edition that requires changing. And, in part, this reinforces one of the major points of the book, *that the content of the curriculum should not focus on the specific, immediate problems of society, which are constantly changing, but on the underlying long-range problems which our students will still have to cope with decades from now.*

Many of the problems discussed herein have gotten worse in the past five years, and none has shown any sign of vanishing. The details have changed, of course. The unemployment rate, for example, is somewhat lower at the moment than in 1975, while the inflation rate is much worse. By the time you read this, the figures will have changed again. But the *problem* remains the same, to the point where the comments on page 33—concerning "obvious" solutions which just increase inflation and make the problem worse—sound prescient.

Indeed, the problem behind *all* the problems is lack of foresight— by governments, by businesses, but most of all by citizens and voters. There are no short-term solutions to long-term problems, and the crises that bedevil us will only grow more complex and more dangerous as long as the public demands quick, painless answers.

But we can hardly expect people to think wisely about the future if their education is focused solely on the past and present. The only place most people will ever learn the necessary skills is in the classroom—*your* classroom. Whether they do or not will be of incalculable importance for tomorrow.

1. Introduction

> "Human history becomes more and more a race between education and catastrophe."—H. G. Wells

The second half of the twentieth century is different from any other period in the history of the human race, different in ways that have important implications for education.

Perhaps the most significant difference is the emergence, in a mere three decades, of multiple threats to the survival of the entire human species.[1] Although we know of some dangers, such as nuclear war or the possibility that genetic engineering will accidentally produce an unstoppable plague, the greatest threat may well be posed by some innocuous and completely unsuspected bit of modern technology. (Who would have guessed only a few years ago that aerosol spray cans might threaten human life?)[2] We have almost learned to live with these dangers, but we should not be blind to the fact that the situation is unique and that the potential for harmful consequences of foolish or short-sighted policies is enormous.

Another unique characteristic of our times is the sharp increase in the rate of social change, both in the United States and globally.[3] Such sustained high rates of change, driven by a burgeoning technology, make planning for the future and coping with long-range problems enormously more difficult, and may be pushing us to the limits of both individual and institutional adaptability.[4]

A third key difference is in the sheer complexity of society. Advanced technology, population growth and urbanization, the internationalization of economics, and high speed travel and communications have tied nations and the institutions within each nation together so tightly that *there are no longer any simple decisions.* A seemingly simple change of policy in one area of one country may cause serious disruption in another area of the same country or in another nation 10,000 miles away.[5]

Finally, there has been a major increase in the need for anticipatory solutions.[6] This is particularly a problem for a society like that of the United States, which has been accustomed throughout its history to ignore problems until they reach a crisis point, and then to react to them with great efficiency. This makes sense, as long as the crises are not severe enough to destroy the entire society. Unfortunately, many of the problems we face today—such as resource depletion, population growth, famine, environmental disruption, and nuclear proliferation—have a fatal combination of two characteristics: the cost of a full-blown crisis is unacceptably high and, in each case, the "point of no return" is passed *before*, sometimes long before, the crisis point is reached. (For example, population growth takes at least 50 years to level off *after* replacement birth rates are achieved.)[7]

What does all this mean for education? It means that schools, if they are to have any relevance to the needs and demands of society, must give careful and explicit attention to the question: "What kind of education will best prepare these students for the world in which they will actually live their adult lives?"

The time lag in education is enormous. To appreciate that lag, we have only to contemplate the fact that, under normal circumstances, *the students in school today will spend most of their lives in the next century*. It is doubtful that they are even being prepared very well by society for what is left of this one. Education which takes that time lag into account is essential for the well-being of our students, for the survival of society, and for the continuing good health and self-respect of the educational profession.

Future-Oriented Education

The educational philosophy based on these principles is known as "futurism." As an educational philosophy, it is still in its infancy, but it is already showing promise as a framework for pulling together many of the piecemeal curricular reforms of the last decade and for providing a coherent curricular complement to "progressive" education.

Futurism questions traditional education on two grounds. First, traditional methods of education tend to produce individuals who are psychologically ill-equipped to cope with a society undergoing continual rapid change. Second, the content of the traditional curriculum is designed to fit the student into the existing society, in spite of the fact that the society (more accurately, the succession of

Introduction

societies) which the student will live in will be quite different—a case of trying to hit a moving target by aiming at it where it is now, rather than where it will be.

A response to the first problem can be found in the efforts of progressive education to produce individuals who are more open, flexible, and inner-directed, since these characteristics are great advantages for coping with a changing environment. But psychological capabilities are only part of the answer, and the great weakness of the progressive movement has been its almost exclusive attention to the *affective* side of education and its failure to develop a strong rationale for reforming the *cognitive* curriculum.[8] Futurism provides such a rationale, and the curriculum which it proposes is called "future studies" or "future-oriented education."

Although there have always been exceptional teachers who have helped students see the connection between what they were learning and the life ahead of them, courses and teaching methods concerned directly with the future are a relatively recent phenomenon. One of the first high school courses on the future was taught by Priscilla Griffiths at Melbourne High School in Florida in 1966–67. The number of teachers involved in developing similar courses or units at the elementary or secondary levels grew gradually to more than a thousand in 1973–74[9] and has increased rapidly since then, partly as a result of a spate of conferences and teacher workshops, and the encouragement of such key spokespersons as Alvin Toffler, Margaret Mead, and Harold Shane.[10]

Three things about the development of futurism and future studies are particularly noteworthy. First, it has been almost exclusively a grass-roots movement, with teachers designing their own units from scratch, and with very little in the way of curriculum materials and "expert" advice available. Second, it has involved a broad spectrum of teachers from all grade levels and subject areas (with emphasis on social studies, history, English, and science). Third, it has also incorporated a wide range of new curricular materials and ideas, including environmental education, international education, technology studies, and career education.

Although futurism is very much concerned with revamping the entire curriculum, only one school so far seems to have attempted this (the Maslow-Toffler School of the Future, in New York, which graduated its first class of high school seniors in June, 1975).[11] As a result, nearly all of the experimentation in future studies has been done by teachers working either alone or with one or two colleagues to develop a separate course on the future (usually as an elective at the secondary level) or to "futurize" an existing course (common at all levels).[12]

How have they fared? The teachers involved have been almost unanimous in reporting the initial skepticism of their colleagues, the very high enthusiasm of the students, and their own strong sense of personal satisfaction, particularly for subsequent courses taught by the same individual.[13] Course descriptions and syllabi indicate that there has been a wide variation in the kind and quality of course content, as one would expect in an experimental, trial-and-error situation. More important than individual successes and failures, however, is the fact that these efforts have collectively provided a rich range of approaches and content areas for other teachers and curriculum developers to work on.

At this point, it may be appropriate to ask how an educational program on the future can have any content at all. There are no true crystal balls and no one can predict the future with accuracy. Indeed, one of the few things we can be fairly sure of concerning the next 50 years is that it will be different from today and full of surprises. If we don't know what the world will be like when our students are adults, how can we prepare them for it?

There are four basic ways this can be done:

- We can provide students with better, more sophisticated ways of thinking about the future.

- Since the sheer complexity of our social and physical environment is a major part of the problem, we can provide students with the skills and concepts needed to understand complex systems.

- Although we can't predict the future, we *can* identify and help students to understand many of the major issues which will—one way or another—shape the future.

- And since continued rapid change is one of the few certainties, we can help students to understand change and to cope with it.

The appropriate emphasis on each of these four approaches naturally varies from situation to situation, and from grade level to grade level. Although it is easier to discuss them separately, as will be done in the next four chapters, it should be kept in mind that they are not four separate instructional topics, but rather a combined set of educational objectives for the entire curriculum.

2. The Alternative Futures Approach

The human race has always had its prophets and seers, but the last two decades have witnessed the development of a new breed of experts on the future. They are called "futurists," and they differ from the astrologers and crystal-ball gazers of the past in two important ways: first, they are almost completely uninterested in making predictions; and second, they try to use rational methods in their profession (which is called "futuristics").[1] In the process, they have developed a set of concepts and techniques which make it possible to think more intelligently about the future.

Futuristics begins with four basic assumptions:

- The future which actually occurs will be determined partly by history and physical reality, partly by chance, and partly by human choice. The relationships among these factors will vary according to the amount of time one is looking ahead and the nature of the choices made.

- At any given moment, therefore, there exists a *range* of alternative futures which might come about. History and physical reality determine which futures are in that range. Chance and human choice will determine which one of those possible futures will actually happen.

- True "freedom of choice" only exists when one understands the full range of options available *and* the possible consequences of each option.

- The purpose of futuristics, therefore, is *not* to predict the future, but rather to improve our understanding of the range of alternative futures which might come about and of the role that both chance and deliberate choice might play in either achieving or avoiding any particular future.[2]

Thus, to the futurist, "the future" is a *zone of potentiality*, rather than "that which is going to happen." Similarly, "knowl-

11

edge about the future" is seen as *knowledge about what is possible*, rather than knowledge about what is certain. A statement about a future possibility (such as its likelihood, the things which would contribute to its happening, or the effect it would have on other events) is known as a *forecast*, and the process of discovering such information is called *forecasting*. Although many forecasting methods are in current use, none of them is self-sufficient. Instead, each needs to be used in combination with others as part of what can be called "the alternative futures approach" to forecasting.

Trends

The first step in the alternative futures approach is to examine the recent past for trends which might give us a clue as to where things are headed.[3] A trend is simply a consistent tendency or pattern of behavior over a period of time. Although trends are easiest to see when represented by numbers plotted on a graph, a trend can be very real without being measurable.

Identifying trends serves two main purposes. First, although the existence of a trend is no assurance that it will continue, it is unlikely that all existing trends will vanish simultaneously.[4] A thorough study of existing trends can therefore give us a good general feeling for what lies ahead.

Second, each trend we identify can be the basis for a number of fruitful questions:

- What are the underlying causes which created the trend in the past?

- How stable are those conditions likely to be in the future?

- What *new* developments are necessary for the continuation of the trend?

- What new developments might alter it?

- Is the trend approaching some saturation point or limit?

- Does it conflict with some other trend?

- Does the trend benefit government, business, or other interest groups, and will they (can they) support the trend if it falters?

- Does the trend have potentially harmful consequences or side-effects?

The Alternative Futures Approach

- Are there likely to be deliberate efforts to halt or alter the trend?
- How easily can the trend be halted and how long would this take?
- How much time is likely to elapse between the appearance of a problem and the point at which the problem becomes a crisis?
- If the trend does not continue, what are the most likely alternatives?

As alternatives to existing trends are identified, they can be subjected to the same set of questions. Often, the analysis of a trend will require little in the way of specialized knowledge. For example, a simple extension of two trends from the 1950's would indicate that, by 1995, the domestic income of the Xerox Corporation would be larger than the entire gross national product of the United States. Common sense is all that is needed to tell us that Xerox would not be able to sustain that kind of growth.[5] In other cases, the questions will not be so simple, and additional resources will be needed.

Expert Opinion

The next step in the alternative futures approach is to obtain as much information as possible about the *future expectations* of individuals whose backgrounds or special talents make them "experts" on a particular subject.[6] The most obvious way to do this is to search the library for relevant books and articles. This is usually a good starting point, but—for all except the narrowest of topics—it will seldom be sufficient. Experts tend to be conservative in print, for fear that speculations about the future will be misinterpreted and treated as if they were predictions; and those speculations which are available are likely to be out of date or buried in jargon. Moreover, there is the sheer immensity of the task; so many different things might have an effect on a particular trend, and vice versa, that it will probably take an expert to tell us what to look for.

Deciding who the "experts" are, and whom to believe when they disagree, can be an extremely difficult problem.[7] Fortunately, we are primarily interested in finding out about *alternative possibilities*, so there is no need to rely on any one definitive answer to a particular question. Instead, the objective should be to sample as many different viewpoints as possible.

Futurists use a variety of techniques for sampling expert opinion, most of which are variations on the *commission* and the *poll*.[8] The advantage of a commission is that it gets a group of experts together for a face-to-face exchange of views, so that each idea is likely to undergo extensive scrutiny. With a poll or questionnaire, on the other hand, each question may receive less careful consideration, but it is possible for many more points of view to be represented.

When using either of these approaches in the classroom, the selection of "experts" will depend more on availability than on true expertise. A carefully drafted questionnaire, for example, can be given to other teachers at the school, taken home to parents, distributed to faculty members at a nearby college or university, or sent to local business or government leaders. For a commission exercise, on the other hand, each student can be assigned a particular part of the general subject to investigate, and then the students themselves can represent the "experts" on the commission.

It is worth emphasizing again that the purpose of all this is not to find out what *will* happen, but to find out what *might* happen. Experts should be asked to suggest as many different alternatives as possible, even those that are relatively unlikely. Each alternative should then be subjected to the same kinds of questions listed above in the section on "Trends": how likely is it to happen? . . . what does it depend on? . . . what consequences would it have? . . . and so on. The result should be a fairly exhaustive listing of alternative possibilities and a good deal of information about how the different possibilities relate to each other.

Alternative Futures

The concluding step in the alternative futures approach is to assemble the information which has been gathered and organize it into "scenarios" or "alternative futures." The assumption behind this process is that some alternative possibilities are more likely to "go together" than others. For example, continued urbanization of the United States would probably be accompanied by a growing dependence on nuclear reactors. A move towards decentralization, on the other hand, is more likely to be associated with the development of alternative energy sources, such as solar power, windmills, and methane digesters.

The Alternative Futures Approach

By examining these kinds of linkages, one can sort the different possibilities into internally consistent clusters, groupings of future events which contain no contradictory pairs. Furthermore, many possible events can occur only after a certain amount of time has elapsed, either from the present or from the occurrence of some other event. This makes it possible to arrange the alternatives in each cluster into one or more fairly plausible sequences. Each sequence, then, describes one *alternative future*.

When professional futurists do this, they may end up with hundreds, or even thousands, of possible alternative futures.[9] Since no one can keep that many alternatives in mind at once, they will generally select about a half dozen of the most distinctively different alternatives to use as a guide for future planning. For educational purposes, fortunately, we can skip the intermediate step and work directly toward developing six or seven alternative futures which are relatively plausible and as different as possible from each other. This means that arbitrary decisions as to what goes with what, and in what order, will have to be made fairly frequently, but the whole task would otherwise become unmanageable.

The optional final element in this process is to convert each alternative future into a "scenario." A scenario (or "future history") is a fictionalized version of an alternative future.[10] It is usually written in the past tense, from the point of view of a character living in some future year and looking back over the events which have occurred between now and then. Adding characters and a sense of drama helps make the alternative future seem more vivid and memorable.

The set of alternative futures produced by this process serves two main functions.[11] First, it acts as a powerful antidote to "the single future trap." Although we may know, in an intellectual way, that many different futures are possible, it is difficult to imagine these futures and, therefore, easy to slip into the habit of relying on *one* particular image of the future. A good, vivid set of alternative futures or scenarios can be an indispensable aid to the imagination in this respect.

Second, a truly diverse set of alternative futures can be used to test the versatility of present plans. All too often, plans for the future are made which would work in a future environment resembling the present, but which fail drastically in the rather different environment that actually comes about. Although there is no way to prove that a particular plan will work in every possible future, it is possible to test plans against a set of alternative futures and to eliminate those which will only work if the future is just right.

From the educational point of view, however, the most important outcome of the alternative futures process is not the set of scenarios, but rather the experience which students gain in a whole way of looking at the future. If, as a result, they acquire the habit of looking ahead, of evaluating alternative possibilities and their consequences, and of trying to find a balance between influencing the future and adapting to it, they will have taken a major step toward gaining better control over their own lives in an uncertain world.

3. Systems, Stability, and Change

One of the most important problems our students will face as adults is the difficulty of making any sense of the complex systems which surround us. Unfortunately, traditional education has been of little help. At best, a course may be devoted to one particular kind of system, such as the economy or the environment. Such courses are valuable, but they do not get to the heart of the problem, which is complexity itself and strategies for coping with it.

An outsider looking at education might well be surprised at this omission. After all, schools are pre-eminently concerned with teaching students how to think better, and one of the most important developments of our time has been precisely in the area of better understanding of complex systems. The name of this development is "general systems theory," and it has radically transformed almost every branch of science—social, biological, and physical.[1] It is essential, for the sake of our students, that it have an equally important place in the curriculum.

General systems theory can get extremely complex, but the basic ideas which are the key to systems thinking are remarkably simple. Two of the most basic are the definition of a "system" and the notion of "feedback."

Systems. Imagine that you have just entered a store and asked for a radio. The clerk finds out what model you want, takes a box off the shelf, and rings up the sale. You open the box and find several pieces of sheet metal, a few knobs, a long piece of wire, and a handful of transistors. Did you get what you asked for?

Clearly, you did not. A radio is more than just a box full of parts. Like any other system, it is *an organized collection of things which interact with each other to function as a unit or whole*. Without organization, interaction, and wholeness, it is a "heap," not a "system."

Classical science assumed that the whole is equal to the sum of the parts and that, therefore, the way to understand the whole is to take it apart and find out what it is made of. Since this approach, called "reductionism," leads to an inability to distinguish between a building and a pile of bricks, or between a human being and a collection of atoms, it has gradually yielded to the systems approach, which assumes: 1) that the whole can be greater than the sum of the parts, with the difference coming from the way the parts are organized; and 2) that we can understand a system only if we know *both* what it is made of and how it is organized.[2]

Since one defining characteristic of a system is that the parts interact to form a larger whole, it follows that a system itself can be one component of a larger system. The larger system, in turn, can be a sub-system of a still larger system, and so on. The one which we choose to call "the system" depends upon where our attention is focused at that particular moment.

Feedback. Part of the definition of a system is that its parts are *interrelated*—that is, each part must either have an influence on or be influenced by other parts of the system, or both. When a component both influences the system and is influenced by it, an interesting situation arises: an alteration of the behavior of the component can alter the behavior of the system which in turn alters the behavior of the component. This is called "feedback," because the behavior of the component "feeds back" through the system to have an effect on the future behavior of the component.[3]

The feedback "loop" can be very simple (A affects B, which affects A, and so on) or quite complex (A affects B, which affects C and D, which both affect E, F, and G, each of which has a different effect on A). Although the new behavior produced by the feedback loop may have almost any relationship to the original change, two patterns are quite common and it is important for students to understand them. "Negative feedback" occurs when the effect of the feedback loop is to *reverse* or *negate* the change in behavior. "Positive feedback" occurs when the effect of the feedback loop is to *support* or *amplify* the change in behavior. Although the two conditions are diametrically opposed, they share two attributes: first, one must understand both in order to understand stability and change in the human environment; second, both behave in "counter-intuitive" ways which are likely to mislead the unwary.

Systems and Stability

Since negative feedback *negates* changes in the system, its effect is to bring the system back to its original condition. As a result, a system which is dominated by a negative feedback loop (or loops) will tend to stabilize itself in spite of changes in the surrounding environment. The pattern which this produces, a kind of automatic and *active* stability in a changing environment, is called "homeostasis."[4]

Perhaps the simplest example of a homeostatic system is the heating system in your home. As long as the weather is cool and the furnace is off, the temperature of the air in the house will gradually drop. When it falls more than a degree or two below the temperature you have set on the thermostat, the thermostat responds by turning the furnace on. The furnace warms the house up until the temperature reaches a point one or two degrees higher than the set temperature, which causes the thermostat to turn the furnace off, which causes the house to cool down, which causes the thermostat to turn the furnace on, and so forth. As a result, the system is able to keep the inside temperature nearly constant whether the outside temperature drops to zero or climbs to the sixties. (And if you add an air-conditioner to the system, it will work year-round at any temperature.)

Having a thermostat in your house is a convenience, but it is not a matter of earth-shaking importance. On the other hand, the thermostat in your body is literally a matter of life and death.[5] One of the inherited blessings of being a mammal is an efficient system for keeping body temperature within narrow limits, regardless of changes in the outside environment. When your body starts to cool down, you shiver, you begin burning off more calories, the blood flow to the body surface is reduced, and you feel uncomfortable enough to look for warmer clothes or a warmer environment. If your body gets too hot, you start to sweat, your skin becomes flushed, and you are likely to have a strong urge to find a cold drink and a spot in the shade. The system normally keeps variations in your body temperature to less than one degree. A variation of five degrees means that you are quite ill, and a ten-degree variation will kill you.

Your bodily thermostat is only one of hundreds of negative feedback loops which keep you alive.[6] The circulatory system alone carries dozens of substances—oxygen, carbon dioxide, water, salt, sugar, urea, amino acids, steroids, hormones, antibodies, clotting agents, and many more—each one of which is closely regulated by one or more negative feedback loops. Negative feedback also governs the physical coordination of our bodies. Without it, you could not stand or walk without falling down, write your name, hit a baseball, eat with knife and fork, drive a car, or do anything else which requires a controlled interaction between your body and the environment.[7] Nor is this enormous dependence on negative feedback restricted solely to bodily processes. Learning of all kinds would be impossible without the correction of inappropriate interpretations or behaviors.[8] And no social organization, from a friendship to an international government, can function without penalties on destructive behaviors.[9]

Problems. When a physical, biological, or social system has the ability to maintain its continuity and adapt to changing conditions, it gets that ability from one or more negative-feedback loops. Negative feedback is therefore a "good thing"—the earth would be a lifeless rock without it—but the persistence and adaptability it produces can also be a problem when we *want* to change such a system. Perhaps the largest part of the problem is not the resistance of the system to change, but rather the "counter-intuitive" nature of the system which leads those who wish to change it to expend their efforts in unfruitful ways.[10]

The furnace-thermostat model again provides a useful example. Imagine that it is a cold winter day, that you are sitting in the living room of a typical house, and that you find it uncomfortably chilly in the room. The living room contains a thermostat (set at 65° F.), a fireplace, and a supply of wood, kindling, and matches. Since the problem is one of being too cold, the "obvious" solution is to create more heat by building a fire. What effect will this have? Oddly enough, it will probably make the room colder! It will certainly have that effect on the rest of the house.

Why is this? First, since the thermostat is set to turn the furnace off when the room temperature rises above 65° F., any extra heat produced by the fireplace will simply cause the furnace to shut down. Even if the fireplace is large enough to keep the living room warm by itself, the rest of the house will get colder and colder, gradually pulling more and more heat away from the living room through the interior walls. Second, to make matters worse, that nice blazing fire is sending large amounts of hot air soaring up the chimney, which pulls cold outside air into the house through the cracks around doors and windows.

Again, the example is trivial, but the principle is extremely important: *the "obvious" solution to a problem controlled by a negative feedback loop will rarely have any impact, except that it will frequently make the problem worse.* The solution instead is to modify the *control element* in the feedback loop. In the example above, almost everyone knows that raising the thermostat setting will make the house warmer (although most people do *not* know that building a fire will make it colder). But in most social issues, the "obvious"—and wrong—intervention may appear to be the *only* possible solution.

One excellent example is rent control. When a city experiences a shortage of rental units, the rents on apartments are likely to increase rapidly. If a large proportion of the population consists of renters, the pressure on the city government to adopt the "obvious" solution—rent controls—may be considerable. Unfortunately, the results are rarely what was intended. Instead of raising rents, the building owners try to reduce costs by cutting back on maintenance and services. Thus, instead of paying more for the same housing value, the renter pays the *same* price for a *reduced* value. In the meantime, rent controls have made the building of new apartments unprofitable, so the housing shortage continues, making it almost impossible to lift the rent controls. If the rent controls are left in place, inflation will eventually drive increased costs to the point where they exceed the income from rents. When this happens, the owner has little choice except to stop all maintenance and let the building fall apart. The building then deteriorates rapidly down to slum conditions and eventually must be condemned, thus reducing the housing supply still further.[11]

In short, the direct solution will make the situation a great deal worse. The alternative is more painful in the short run, but has the advantage of actually solving the problem. If rent controls are avoided, the high rentals will make apartment buildings much more attractive to investors, thus precipitating a building boom. This will almost invariably produce an oversupply of apartments, which in turn will drive the rents back down. Since this kind of oversupply and undersupply "boom/bust" cycle is likely to continue (just as the thermostat kept the house temperature cycling a few degrees above and below the target temperature), the city may then decide to prevent the *next* shortage from occurring by subsidizing the construction of new buildings. By variations in the amount of the subsidy, a constant, slight oversupply of apartments can be assured, thus keeping rents low. (This will also be *cheaper* in the long run, since a city's income depends on its real-estate tax base; slums and abandoned buildings contribute less in taxes than they cost in city services.)

Pursuing the "obvious" solution does not always make things actively worse, of course, but it can often do just as much harm by diverting attention and energy from workable solutions. For example, the ecologically-minded public has put a tremendous amount of time and effort over the last decade into the voluntary recycling of cans, bottles, and paper. All of this effort has only a trivial effect on the recycling problem, and the effect which it does have lasts only as long as the enthusiasm for volunteer effort continues.[12]

The "thermostat" in this case is the Congress. If one quarter of the effort which has gone into recycling drives had gone into raising funds and lobbying Congress, bills could have been passed quite easily to ban "one-way" containers and to remove the rate penalties for shipping recyclable materials. The effect on the problem would not only have been much greater, it would have been an enduring effect.

Systems and Change

Since negative feedback involves continual adaptation to the environment, it produces a kind of change as well as stability. This is particularly true when human beings are part of the feedback loop. For example, the thermostat controls the heating system in your house to keep the temperature near the desired level, but the thermostat is also part of larger feedback loops in which *you* determine what the desired level is, according to comfort, economics, and attitudes. The effect of these larger feedback loops was seen in 1973 and 1974, when temperatures were reduced in homes across the United States as an adaptation to the Arab oil boycott.

Like negative feedback, positive feedback can produce both stability and change (although the latter dominates). The kind of positive feedback which tends to produce stability comes about when a reward is given for behavior which might not otherwise be repeated. Although this approach can be used to build complex new behaviors from simple, or even random, components (as the Skinnerian psychologists do in training a pigeon to play ping-pong), it is basically a way of insuring the continuation of existing behaviors.

The change-producing kind of positive feedback occurs when the result of an action is to make the system *more capable* of producing the same action in the future. The most familiar example is the compound interest earned by money in a bond or savings account. If, for example, you invest $1000 in a bond which pays 10%, you will earn $100 during the first year, giving you a total of $1100 at the end of the year. Since you have increased the amount of money you hold by 10%, you have also increased your capacity to earn more money with it by the same amount—10%. Thus your earnings for the second year would be $110, instead of $100.[13]

Such situations, where each unit of growth increases the capacity for further growth, produce a characteristic pattern of increase which is called an "exponential growth" curve. Students need to understand such curves for two important reasons. First, nearly all of the driving force behind the high rate of change in our society comes directly or indirectly from just three exponential curves: population growth, economic growth, and scientific and technological progress. Second, as was the case with negative feedback, exponential growth produces effects which are surprising and "counter-intuitive"—contrary to the normal expectations of someone not familiar with how exponential growth works.[14]

To get a feeling for the power and unexpected nature of exponential growth, suppose that you have a classroom which holds 30 students comfortably, is a bit crowded with 40 students, and is bursting at the seams with 50 students. If you begin with two students and add two more students each day, you will receive plenty of warning between the 16th and 20th days that your classroom is becoming overcrowded. If, on the other hand, you begin with two students and *double* the number of students each day, you will have a relatively comfortable 32 students on the fifth day and an absolutely impossible 64 students on the sixth day!

Most people (and most institutions) depend upon gradually increasing symptoms of stress to warn of an approaching danger or overload, but an exponential growth situation will not produce such danger signals until the crisis point has very nearly been reached.[15] The problem is compounded if a process producing exponential growth cannot be stopped in less than one "doubling time"; such situations should be treated with profound suspicion if there is any possibility of harmful consequences.

There are three basic points which students need to grasp in order to understand and cope with exponential growth patterns:

- Any quantity which increases by a fixed percentage per unit of time is said to be growing exponentially.

- Every exponential growth curve has a characteristic *doubling time*. If something growing exponentially takes ten years to double, it will double again in the second ten years, and again in the third ten years, and in each decade thereafter.

- The approximate doubling time can be found by dividing the percentage growth rate into the number 70 (the "Rule of 70"). In other words, something growing at 1% per year will take 70 years to double; at 2% it would take 35 years, at 5% it would take 14 years, at 10% it would take only 7 years, and so on.[16]

There is, of course, no guarantee that a particular growth rate will remain constant, but the "rule of 70" at least provides a handy means for estimating what the consequences would be if it did. For example, students encountering the current growth rate for world population—two percent per year—are likely to be unimpressed by such a low number.[17] If they use the rule of 70 to convert that to a doubling time, however, they will discover what a two percent growth rate means: *everything* involved in the support of population, including food production, energy supplies, education, housing, and medical facilities, will have to be doubled in just 35 years in order for the world's population to be no worse off than it is today. This provides a much better picture of the consequences of the trend and, indeed, provides the basis for a discussion of whether or not the continuation of the trend is possible.[18]

Complex Systems

Up until now, we have been looking at individual feedback loops and their influence for stability and change. In the real world, however, feedback loops rarely occur by themselves; instead, they are likely to occur in complex networks of interrelated feedback loops, both positive and negative. The *systems approach* is to attempt to identify the major linkages in such networks, in order to get a better grasp of the behavior of the whole.

For example, Figure 1 shows some of the more important relationships between industrialization (bottom), natural resources (left), food production, pollution, health, and education (right), and population (top). Even without precise information about the effect indicated by each arrow, the diagram allows us to get a feeling for the "pattern" of influences in the system. From the human point of view, the important items in the diagram are the ones which contribute to the quality of life: the output of material goods per person, the amount of food per person, the level of pollution, the level of health and education, and the average life span.

With the exception of pollution, each of these is increased by an increase in the output of material goods and decreased by an in-

Systems, Stability, and Change

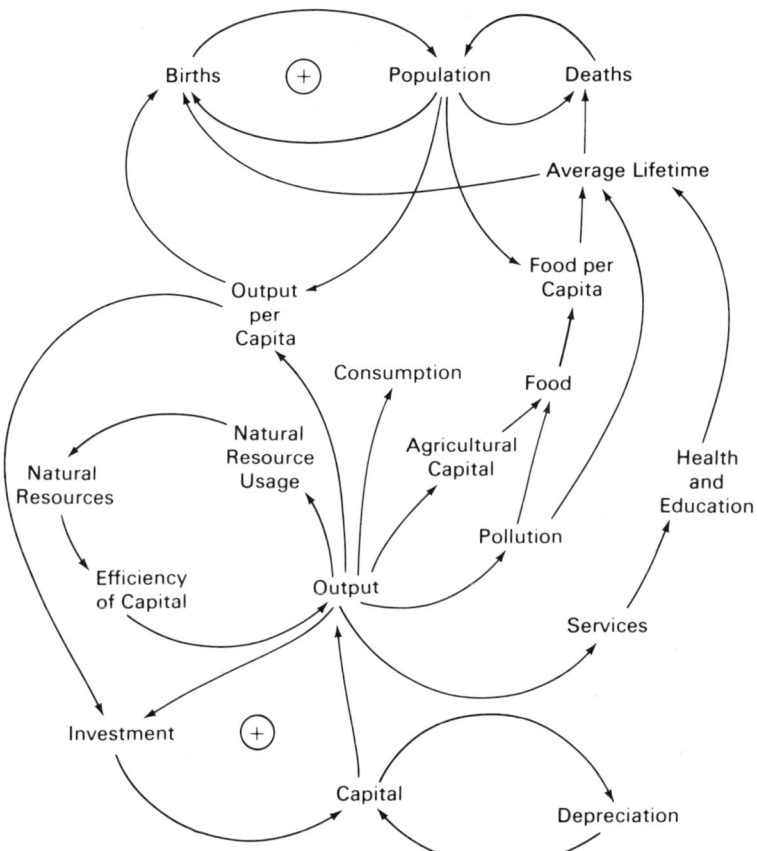

Figure 1.
Basic Interactions Between Population Growth and Capital Accumulation. (Based on Randers and Meadows, "The Carrying Capacity of the Globe," *Sloan Management Review*, Winter 1972.) Used by permission.

crease in population. It would seem, therefore, that the situation will keep getting better as long as the positive feedback loop of industrial capital is stronger than the positive feedback loop of population—and this is the reasoning behind the continuing efforts toward "economic development." But the model also warns that an increase in output produces more pollution (which reduces the food supply and the average life span) and consumes more natural resources (which eventually increases the cost of the resources and reduces the efficiency of capital and the amount of goods produced).

Even this general and qualitative kind of analysis of the structure

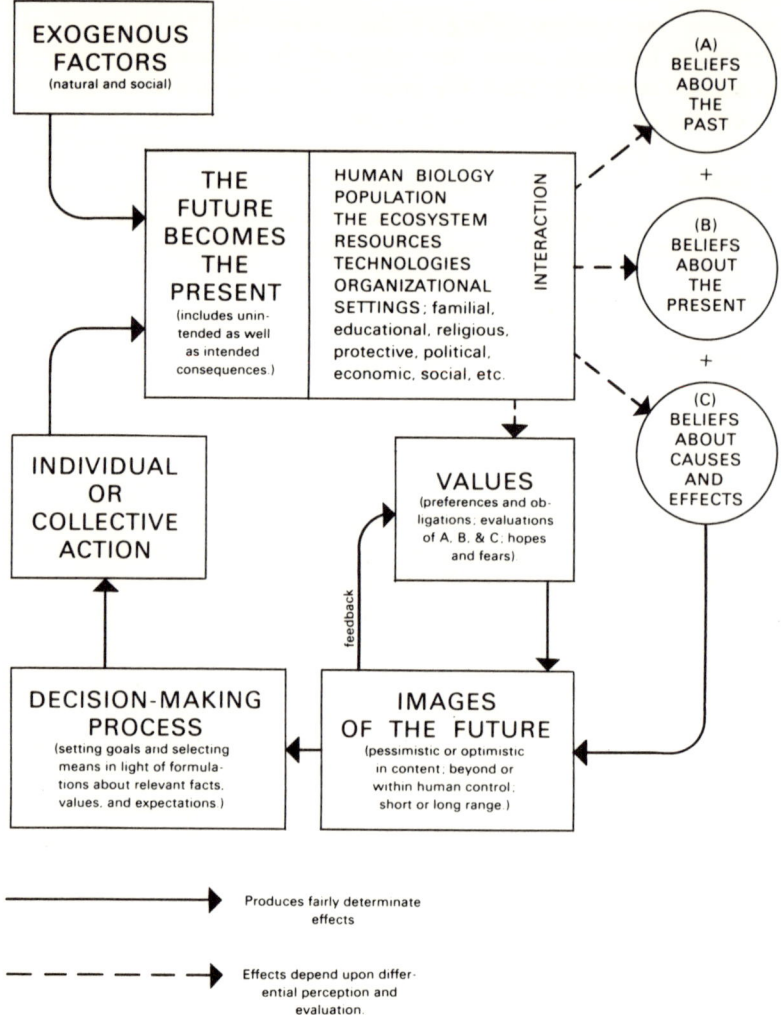

Figure 2.
"Cybernetic-Decisional Model of Social Change," from *The Sociology of the Future* by Wendell Bell and James A. Mau, editors. © 1971 by Russell Sage Foundation, New York. Reprinted by permission.

of a system can be enormously helpful in developing good judgment and intuition about the effects of possible changes on the system. If a fairly good estimate can be made of the relationship between each element of a system and the other elements which indirectly influence it, then it is possible to use the model both to

Systems, Stability, and Change

improve our understanding of the system and to generate alternative forecasts about the future of the system. Typically, a computer is used to trace the impact of any particular change (or combination of changes) as it works its way through the entire system. As in the alternative futures approach described in Chapter 2, a wide variety of possible changes can be proposed, with the results of each change or combination of changes becoming one of a set of alternative possibilities for the future of the system.[19]

The Human Factor

Systems thinking is an important element in future-oriented education because it provides students with the mental tools they need to understand the variety of complex systems which make up the human environment. But even a highly developed understanding of the physical/biological/ecological/political/economic /social macro-system, in which we all must function, can be misleading if human beings are seen as trapped within the same feedback structure which controls all the other elements.[20]

The difference between human and natural systems stems from the unique human capacity for imagining the future. A thermostat can only *react* to what is happening at the moment; human beings can *pre-act* to what they think will or might happen. This introduces a new crucial element to the system, a new kind of loop which depends on *feed-forward* instead of feedback (see Figure 2). It is the awareness both of the nature of complex systems and of the unique role that human intelligence plays in those systems which constitutes the true systems perspective.[21]

4. Key Issues

The two preceding chapters have been concerned with the conceptual side of future-oriented education, emphasizing more productive ways of looking at the future and of coping with complexity. But future-oriented education has a content side as well. In one sense, that content can be described as everything, since a good education for the future ought first of all to be a wide-ranging education. In another sense, however, it is clear that some issues are going to have a much larger effect on the future, whichever way they turn out, than others. An understanding of those issues can go a long way toward providing students with an understanding of the era and their place in it.

No list of such issues could possibly be complete, for surprises are one of the few certainties for the future. However, although many issues will be omitted which should have been included, it is possible to prepare such a list with reasonable confidence that few of the items included should have been omitted. Since a thorough treatment of any one of these issues would require at least a chapter, if not a whole volume, what follows is instead a potpourri of key topics from which appropriate selections can be made for use in the curriculum.

Global Problems

War and Peace. Although the threat of nuclear war no longer dominates public concern the way it did in the 50's and 60's, a good case can be made that it is still *the* overriding issue of our time. Despite 15 years of disarmament talks and the achievement of massive overkill by both sides, the arms race between the super-powers continues. Meanwhile, the long-feared proliferation of nuclear nations has begun. China and India have recently joined the "nuclear club," while the nations which have or are acquiring the capacity to build nuclear weapons now include West Germany, Spain, the Republic of China (Taiwan), South Korea, Japan, Israel, Egypt, Libya,

Brazil, Argentina, Pakistan, and South Africa.¹ Each additional nation increases the risk that nuclear weapons will be used and reduces the prospects for an effective world peace-keeping system or for a disarmament agreement.

Population and Food. By 1974, Soviet grain purchases, poor harvests in parts of Asia, and the Arab oil boycott had driven world food stocks down to a critical three-week supply.² An emergency World Food Conference, held in Rome in November 1974, produced a great deal of rhetoric and no action.³ Many Third World nations took the opportunity to denounce population controls and to castigate the United States, the world's largest exporter of food, for not producing more. Since that time, nothing meaningful has been done to establish food stockpiles or other measures for famine relief.⁴ Food production is losing the race with the population explosion, and a massive famine within the decade seems probable. The main question remaining is whether famine will come in a single global disaster, or whether it will come as a chronic series of regional famines. In either case, the response of the United States will be a critical factor in determining the extent of both the famine and the subsequent disruption.

Resources and Development. The gap between rich and poor nations continues to bedevil the consciences of the wealthy. To many, the solution is economic development. Four problems arise: 1) for most of the poorest nations, the growth of the population equals or exceeds the growth of the economy, wiping out any per capita gains;⁵ 2) it is seldom recognized that, if two economies are growing at the same rate, the *gap* between the two economies will also grow at that same rate;⁶ 3) latecomers to development must compete for increasingly scarce and expensive supplies of natural resources, making development much more difficult; 4) the earth lacks the resources and the pollution-absorbing capacity which would be needed to support a situation in which all nations are developed to the economic level of Western Europe. Thus, economic development is likely to prove a false hope for many of the poorest fourth of the world's peoples, particularly if birthrates remain at current levels. Yet the moral dilemma remains, and will remain as long as there is abject poverty side-by-side with extraordinary wealth.

The Environment. The fourth key issue affecting the future of the world is the endangerment of the global environment. Polluted air and polluted water pay no attention to national boundaries. A species of whale driven to extinction is a loss to all humankind.

Even environmental problems which appear to be strictly local in their effects may depend upon international solutions. If one nation refuses to impose expensive pollution controls on its industry, it can produce products for export more cheaply; other nations which depend on exports of those same products will then be forced to allow the same levels of pollution or find themselves unable to compete.[7]

The complexity of any natural environment gives it a great deal of resistance to human abuse, but that same complexity makes it impossible for us to know in advance how much abuse the environment can take. As a result, every elimination of a habitat or species, every introduction of a new artificial chemical, and every increase in the demands we are already making on the environment represents an increased risk of unknowingly crossing some threshhold which will cause the system to collapse.[8] It has happened before. Much of the Sahara Desert is human-made; much of the "fertile crescent" is barren rock and sand; the greatness of ancient Greece depended on now-vanished forests; and the great Mayan civilization appears to have collapsed when it destroyed the fertility of the soil.[9] The difference this time is that the effects may well be global. One of the most important tasks for the next fifty years will be the development of ecologically benign technologies and of global monitoring and enforcement processes.

The Economy

The economic well-being of any society depends directly on how wisely and efficiently it uses its supplies of labor, land, natural resources, and industrial capital. The free-enterprise approach to these objectives is based on two assumptions: 1) since the carrot is more effective than the stick, society as a whole will benefit if individuals are directly rewarded for increasing the value to society of their own labor or other resources; and 2) the best way to determine the value of something to society at a particular moment is to find out what the members of the society are willing to pay for the existing supply in a free, competitive market.[10] The result is a highly decentralized system, based on the law of supply and demand and the principle of private ownership of labor and capital. It has been an enormously efficient system, but not one without problems.

Short-sightedness. The system is inherently short-sighted, for two reasons. First, it requires the "prudent investor" to *discount future values.* If the return on an investment is 10% each year, the original investment will increase 16-fold in 28 years. An investment which would be worth $1,000 in 28 years is therefore worth only $62 today. As a result, the value of the next generation's environment is discounted almost entirely by the present market.[11] No society can survive if it does this. Ways must be found to insure that tomorrow's resources are not destroyed for pennies today, ways which will include the "grandchild vote" in economic decision-making.

Second, the economy is short-sighted because many producers do not have to pay the full costs of producing their products, and thus have an incentive to invest resources in ways which represent a loss, rather than a gain, to the society.[12] Most of these "external costs"—in the form of air and water polluted, renewable resources destroyed, fertile land paved over, and so on—are really *future costs*, debts incurred in the process of making soap or steel or subdivisions which will be paid by the next generation in the form of lost opportunities and a degraded environment. In effect, external costs represent a special subsidy given only to those who *harm* the society. Even business would gain from elimination of these subsidies, since they are a major source of business's bad public image.

Cycles. Another basic characteristic of market economies is their tendency toward cycles of growth and recession.[13] This cyclical pattern is typical of almost all systems which are stabilized by negative feedback loops; to use our over-worked prototype of negative feedback for yet another example, the thermostat described in Chapter 3 did not keep the house temperature *constant*, but rather controlled it in a regular series of cycles within one or two degrees on either side of the target temperature. In the case of the economy, the basic negative loop (connecting inventories and production) is superimposed on an exponential growth curve generated by the basic positive loop of capital investment. Together, these tend to produce a cycle of high growth and no-growth (recession), rather than a thermostat-like alternation of growth and negative growth (depression).

By itself, the normal business cycle would not be a particular problem. The difficulty arises because of the growing public intolerance of the no-growth part of the cycle, and their insistence that the government *do something* to prevent it.[14] This is analogous to insisting that the thermostat keep the temperature *precisely* at 70° F.; when such systems are built for special laboratories, the cost may run upwards of $100,000.[15] The search for ways of fine-tuning the economy has proven similarly expensive, without achieving the desired precision. As a result, legislators have increasingly fallen back on "obvious" solutions—such as wage-price controls, huge deficits, and erratic shifts in the money supply—all of which cause inflation, which simply makes the cyclical problem worse.[16] Unless the public can be reconciled to occasional periods of less than normal growth, it is likely that such efforts will eventually destroy the existing free-enterprise economy.

Job Obsolescence. Of all of the effects which rapid technological change has on the economy, perhaps the one with the most impact on education is the rapid turnover in the content of work. If current trends continue, 25% of the *kinds* of jobs which exist today will not exist in 10 years, and 25% of the jobs ten years from now will be ones which do not exist today.[17] Even where the same job title is retained, the content of the job may change considerably. One problem facing education, then, is how to prepare young people for careers which may involve abrupt shifts and nearly continuous requirements for learning new skills. The traditional forms of vocational education are often worse than useless in this respect, because they take time during the critical adolescent period away from learning of more general and adaptable skills. The only solution is a broad form of career education which acquaints students with the kaleidoscopic pattern of shifting employment and prepares them with a good base for continued learning.

Unemployment and Welfare. As this is being written, 55% of all Americans over 16 have jobs—close to a record—yet the unemployment rate stands at 9%. How can the employment rate and the unemployment rate both be so high at the same time? The answer is that the percentage of the adult population *wanting* to work has grown dramatically, for three basic reasons. First, agribusiness and the civil rights movement have pushed many of the under-employed rural poor into the job market. Second, the post-war boom babies are now between 16 and 30, which boosts the percentage of single adults and active work-seekers. Finally, delayed marriages, reduced birth rates, the women's liberation movement, and the increasing intellectualization of work have drawn a growing proportion of women, both married and single, into the workplace. The result has been a substantial increase in the potential labor force, much of it occurring within the last 10 to 15 years.[18]

Any economy has a dual purpose: to produce goods and services, and to provide jobs so that people can earn the right to a share of what is produced. By historical standards, the U.S. economy is doing extremely well as a source of jobs. The question remains as to whether it can do enough better to accommodate all who want jobs. Is it possible to have meaningful work outside the home for 60% or 70% of the population? If not, what provision can be made for those who want to work and cannot find jobs? The traditional solution would have been to exclude married women from the marketplace. This is impossible and undesirable for social reasons, and it would also be suicidal for economic reasons. With our society headed toward a knowledge economy and heavily dependent on research and innovation for survival, women represent half the brain power and creativity available to the nation.

The old solution did have one advantage, however, in that the wage-earner provided "transfer payments" directly to those excluded from employment, without government intervention. Since people tend to choose spouses with similar educational levels,[19] there is a growing tendency in the knowledge economy for the nuclear family to have either all of its adult members employable, or none; the result is to *separate* the employed from the unemployable, both personally and in terms of social class. Our current strategy is for the government to tax those who do hold jobs to provide for those who don't. The system by which this is accomplished is wasteful, expensive, and coercive and degrading for the recipient. An alternative strategy is badly needed, whether it consists of a straightforward negative income tax, or a new form of economic unit equivalent to the old extended family, or some completely different approach.

Growth. The final economic issue, and perhaps the most important one in the long run, is the problem of growth itself. Any industrial economy depends upon the supply of energy and other raw materials available to it and on the capacity of the environment to absorb its pollutants. There are good indications that we are near, and perhaps beyond, the levels of resource demand and pollution production which can be sustained over the long term.[20] Even if nuclear fusion is developed as an almost unlimited and pollution-free alternative to fossil fuels, the growth in energy demand would eventually be limited by the total heating of the earth's atmosphere. Other resource limitations can be stretched by substitution and extensive recycling, and environmental limits can be avoided by reducing the amount of pollution generated by each unit of production. But these measures also represent increasing costs and would take considerable time to develop and implement.

The results are likely to be falling returns on industrial capital and, provided no particular limit is exceeded in the meantime, a gradual reduction in the growth of the industrial sector of the economy. Although the knowledge and service sectors of the economy can take up some of the slack, productivity gains are harder to achieve in these areas, making a shift to slow-to-no-growth likely for the economy as a whole. Although no-growth might be desirable for many non-economic reasons, among them the opportunity it would give the developing nations to catch up, it poses a serious threat to the economic stability of all industrialized nations. The expectation of future growth is the mainspring which drives these economies, and nobody has yet provided a satisfactory description of a successful equilibrium economy and how it would work. Solving this problem may be the most important economic challenge of the next half-century.

Politics and Government

The American form of government is the oldest, the largest, and still one of the most successful examples of *applied systems design* in the world.[21] Free public elections, the decentralized system of local, state, and national governments, and the system of checks and balances (so frequently referred to in civics classes) add up to a balanced set of interlocking negative feedback loops. The result, in theory, is a system which is flexible and responsive, yet carefully limited. Each part has functions of its own and also stands ready to check abuses elsewhere in the system, with the whole system subject to the guidance of an informed, skeptical, and unintimidated public. In practice, it has proven to be a system which does not so much prevent abuse as react to it. Nevertheless, and in spite of the problems which will be discussed below, it has proven to be an exceptionally stable form of government and one that provides near-maximum personal liberty for the average citizen.

Corruption of Feedback Channels. The Constitution lays out the basic design for our government, but the Bill of Rights is what makes it work. No individual or group in power likes to hear criticism, and even the best-intentioned leaders can be convinced that the national security depends on keeping secrets from the public, controlling an "irresponsible" press, and intimidating "dissidents" and "radicals." The articles of the Bill of Rights and the impeachment articles in the Constitution have, with a few notable lapses, functioned fairly well to counter such temptations.

Modern technology, however, is making it much more difficult to keep government from controlling the information flow or coercing the citizenry. As Watergate and its aftermath have made clear, a substantial number of government agencies have the capacity to spy on citizens who have broken no laws, collect massive dossiers on them, and use the regulatory powers of government to "punish" them for their political beliefs. Despite the successful outcome, Watergate represented the worst Constitutional crisis the country has faced since the Civil War. As the powers of government increase, we urgently need to put more modern and powerful restraints on government, bringing the spirit of the Bill of Rights up to date. Otherwise, the next crisis may well be the last one.

Money and Politics. In addition to increasing the risks of governmental coercion, modern technology has also greatly increased the political influence of large sums of money. The *illegal* use of money to buy votes or bribe politicians has always existed, of course. But television, radio, and the extensive use of computers have now made it possible—and even necessary—for a candidate to use large sums of money *legally* to influence public opinion. Some halting steps have already been taken in the direction of controls on campaign contributions and spending, but further controls and a great deal of vigilance will be needed to insure that future elections are fought, not bought.

An Informed Public. No democracy can survive if its citizens do not understand the essential issues before it. Despite increasing years of education, the American public is becoming less well informed compared to the growing complexity of the problems it faces. Four tendencies on the part of the public are likely to prove increasingly troublesome: 1) insistence that government cure every social ill; 2) insistence on immediate solutions; 3) short-sightedness and the refusal to accept present penalties for future gains; and 4) an insistence on "obvious" solutions, despite repeated indications that they do not work.[22]

The public response to the energy crisis has provided an excellent recent example of all four tendencies. Despite the nearly unanimous warning of scientists, policy analysts, and politicians of both parties that the energy situation is critical, the public refuses to believe that a problem exists as long as gas is available at the pumps.[23] Consequently, Congress has been unable to pass even minimum taxes to promote conservation and prevent future shortages.[24] A refusal to act to prevent future crises eventually leads to crisis overload and disaster. It can only be hoped that, before that point is reached, a combination of education and repeated experience with crises which could have been prevented, but were not, will induce the public to look more closely at the issues and the possible alternatives.

Centralization. Partly as a result of the complexity of the problems we face and partly as a result of the four tendencies cited above, another threat to our political system is the tenacious growth of governmental bureaucracies, particularly at the federal level. In the first place, the sheer size of government poses a danger to a free society when one-fifth of the work-force is on the government payroll. In the second place, centralization and bureaucratization are extremely inefficient ways of managing a society. The Interstate Commerce Commission is an excellent example of what a government regulatory agency can do to destroy a competitive market and create chaos and inefficiency in the area it is supposed to be regulating.[25] The whole concept of bureaucratic regulation needs to be seriously reconsidered, and replaced wherever possible by "framework" governance, using the tax system and the courts to establish an environment in which the *desired* behavior is also the most profitable behavior.[26]

Values and Diversity. It is not sufficient for the citizens of a democracy to be well-informed; they must also share some minimum of basic values and a willingness to get along with others with different backgrounds or points of view. Since 1960, the overt social consensus in the United States has been increasingly fragmented.[27] Bitter moral disputes, over issues such as censorship, abortion, and drug use, have been forced into the political arena with increasing frequency. If this continues, Americans will have to learn how to live with and tolerate a variety of life-styles and moral perspectives, in the way that we have learned to tolerate a broad spectrum of political ideologies. Nevertheless, the development of a new consensus would be highly desirable, since it would make concerted action on many of the other problems facing the country more possible.[28]

Equity and Social Justice. Perhaps the most fundamental area of change in the social consensus has been on the question, "What is *fair*?" For a long time, the official consensus in this country was that "fairness" consisted of *equality before the law* and *distributive justice* based on the notion that individuals should be rewarded in proportion to their contributions.[29] As the country moved away from an agrarian economy, it became increasingly apparent that the ability to earn a living depended on more than the individual's native ability and industriousness. If the economy did not create enough jobs to go around, or if some individuals were denied the education needed to get a job, some would be left to starve through no fault of their own.

As a result, "fairness" has been expanded to include 1) the right to a minimum standard of living for those unable to work and 2) the notion of equality of opportunity.[30] Both concepts are still in the process of being defined. For example, equal opportunity obviously means a ban on all kinds of invidious discrimination. Does it also mean an equal right to the same educational resources or does it mean an equal chance at the same educational results? Does it make a difference if the child's background is deprived partly as a result of past discrimination by the society?

The courts appear to be headed for a compromise position on educational equality, similar to the compromise on income: all students have an equal right to the same educational resources, except that each child has the right to whatever additional resources are needed to bring that child up to a minimum acceptable level of education (or the highest level the child can attain). Similar standards seem to be emerging in a variety of other areas, such as health care and legal services, in addition to education and income.

This two-fold standard of equality—an equal right to an acceptable minimum and an equal opportunity to compete for more—may be the most effective compromise that can be made between the need for incentives and the need for equality. Unfortunately, it is also subject to endless controversy. What is meant by an "acceptable" minimum? To how many different areas of life should the standard be applied? It also leaves unanswered the question of what to do about intergroup inequality and about very large accumulations of wealth. There will be no easy answers to any of these controversies, but a concerted effort to find acceptable answers is essential if the United States is to regain the good will and allegiance of many citizens who now feel excluded or unfairly treated.

Science and Technology

Pro or Con? Ever since the first demonstration that a hunting club could be used to brain a neighbor as well as an antelope, people have been ambivalent about new developments in science and technology. Scientific progress has brought unquestionable benefits in this century, with medicine and communications as outstanding examples, but it has also created an appalling capacity for species self-destruction and a continually increasing rate of social change. How should we feel about this? It is too late to turn back to some pre-technological Eden. Nearly four billion people would die if we made the attempt. It is also too late to remain where we are. The current environmental-technological base for our civilization is inherently transitory, since it depends on consuming the environment and resources which make it possible in the first place.[31] Furthermore, many of the social problems created by proliferating technology will require further developments in technology for their solution.

The continued development of science and technology is essential to our survival. This does not mean, however, that we should give it our unquestioning support. Indeed, the very potency of the technologies which we need in order to solve our current problems guarantees that new, more severe problems will arise from those same technologies unless they are strictly controlled. The problem is to keep tight rein on harmful technologies without, at the same time, putting deadening restrictions on the scientific research so urgently needed.

Energy. One of the two most basic technical problems we need to solve is that of finding an acceptable substitute for our dependence on petroleum and natural gas, which will last three decades at the most, even with conservation.[32] Coal is plentiful and cheap, but expensive new technologies are needed to extract it and burn it without unacceptable damage to the environment.[33] The same is true for oil shale and tar sands, except that the costs are likely to be even higher.[34] Hydroelectric, tidal, and geothermal power are limited to specific locations and cannot contribute much of the overall energy supply; geothermal power also poses some technical and environmental problems.[35] Atomic fission is both dirty and dangerous; no sane society would undertake the security risks and the 25,000 year waste management obligations it entails.[36] Hydrogen fusion would be a virtually inexhaustible and relatively non-polluting power source, but it may take 30 years or more to develop a working technology.[37] Finally, solar energy is an excellent source for space heating and cooling, but both it and wind power are intermittent (which requires elaborate storage systems) and still too expensive to use as primary sources of electricity.[38]

Out of this range of options, the best bets for research would appear to be: 1) systems for burning coal cleanly and/or for converting it to clean gaseous or liquid fuels; 2) efficient storage systems for intermittent power sources, like solar and wind energy; 3) better solar collectors and electrical conversion systems; and 4) a maximum long-term effort on fusion power. In the meantime, all new buildings should be designed for maximum self-sufficiency, using solar and wind power wherever possible, and all stationary generating plants should be designed or adapted for the cleanest possible use of coal. If the research efforts are successful, these measures *might* allow us to conserve sufficient oil and natural gas to make it through the changeover period to other energy sources without a devastating energy depression.

Environmental Technology. The necessary complement to solving the energy problem is the need to design an environmentally sound technological economy. Such a system must meet four basic requirements: 1) to save energy and recycling costs, all durable goods should be designed for the maximum possible lifespan and ease of recycling; 2) all non-renewable resources and all human-made compounds which are not biodegradable must be restricted to use within tightly closed recycling loops; 3) disposal of biodegradable wastes must be carefully limited to the long-term handling capacity of the environment; and 4) all natural wastes must be returned to the soil along with whatever additional minerals are needed to maintain the soil in its most fertile condition.[39]

These requirements pose problems which are only partly technical, since their solution will require extensive political action and restructuring of the economy. Nevertheless, they cannot be solved at all unless the technical parts of the problems have been dealt with. Extensive recycling, for example, would require everything from improved versions of current pollution controls and chemical recovery systems to methods for "coding" plastics and metal alloys which would allow a garbage sorting machine to identify their chemical compositions.

One of the more promising prospects for reducing the total load on the environment is the possibility of designing nearly self-sufficient residential housing. The objective would be to group between 10 and 100 residences into an "ecological condominium" which would generate all of its own power, compost all of its own organic garbage and wastes, recycle both wastes and water through a carefully balanced greenhouse ecology, and harvest most of its food supply from that same system.[40] The result would be a community which was dependent on the outside world only for supplemental food supplies (and supplemental water if wells are impossible), manufactured goods, and trash collection. If such systems became widespread, they would greatly reduce the heavy environmental load imposed by the elaborate networks we have set up for distributing energy, food, and water and for disposing of garbage and sewage. (As a valuable bonus, our current vulnerability to malfunctions or sabotage of these networks would be greatly reduced—a point which will be appreciated by those who have lived through a prolonged blackout or garbage strike.)

Computers, etc. The standard of living of any society depends in large part on its productivity, the extent to which the existing technology multiplies the productive value of the average person's labor. A substantial portion of the productivity gains in our society over the last 15 years have come from a single area of technology: computers. The capacity and flexibility of these machines has expanded at a dizzying rate, while their cost and size has dropped just as fast.[41]

The dangers of a computerized society are well recognized;[42] the benefits to individuals are only now being realized. Even a very simple computer, such as the pocket calculators which have taken the United States by storm in the last few years, can save an astounding amount of drudgery (and error).[43] As another example, it is estimated that an automobile carburetor equipped with a micro-computer would cost about the same as a catalytic converter, reduce pollutants just as well, and increase gas mileage in the process.[44] At the other end of the spectrum is the promise of a desk-sized unit including a powerful home computer and communications terminal along with the entire contents of the Library of Congress in storage for ready recall.[45] In short, the computer is likely to have a more powerful impact on the individual in our society than any other single branch of our technology, but it can be an impact for either good or evil. It is up to us to decide which—and to enforce the decision.

Biological Engineering. Ever since the discovery of DNA and the genetic code from which all living organisms are constructed, the potential has existed for learning how to manipulate the code and create organisms to order. In 1974, this possibility became a reality. New techniques permitted researchers to deliberately break sections out of the DNA for one organism and patch these sections into the DNA for another.[46] The dangers are so great of accidentally creating an entirely new disease organism to which human beings would have no resistance that scientists around the world declared a moratorium on such research for several months to reassess the techniques and assure that stringent precautions were being taken. Such techniques have great potential benefits, both as pure research in the effort to find out how life works, and as approaches to improving agricultural productivity by creating better plants and livestock and by providing means to make exact genetic duplicates of superior stock. But the potential for abuse is equally great, ranging from the foolish (babies designed-to-order) to the exceptionally grave (vastly more devastating forms of biological warfare).

○ ○ ○ ○ ○ ○ ○ ○ ○ ○ ○

The list could go on and on. Of necessity, the choices and their descriptions are somewhat subjective, but at least they represent a starting point in the search for a curriculum which focuses on the critical issues of tomorrow. The more students know about these critical issues, and the choices, values, preconditions, and possible consequences which they entail, the better prepared they will be to understand the future and to act responsibly as citizens of the future.

5. The Psychology of the Future

In his book, *Future Shock*, Alvin Toffler brings together a great deal of material describing the extent of social change in the United States and its impact on the individual. Essentially, his argument is 1) that the rate of change in the average individual's personal environment is very high; 2) that, above an optimum level for each individual, additional amounts of change exact a demonstrable cost in physical and mental health and well-being; and 3) that individuals not prepared to cope with extensive changes in society increasingly find themselves left behind to become victims of "future shock." After reviewing the progressively incapacitating symptoms of this malady, Toffler makes a number of recommendations for its prevention. Foremost among these is the prescription he summarized in Cervantes' dictum, "Forewarned forearmed!" An event which is completely unexpected can have a stunning effect; if it has at least been considered in advance as a possibility, much of the shock is eliminated when it actually occurs.[1]

The preceding three chapters have summarized some of the most basic cognitive skills and content areas for a future studies curriculum aimed at forewarning students of what may lie ahead and giving them the ability to continue to look ahead on their own. But a true future-oriented education needs to do more than just provide a cognitive antidote to future shock. The ability to cope with change depends as well on the individual's psychological orientation and attitudes toward the future. To the extent that education can foster more adaptive personalities and more functional attitudes, it needs to do so.

Future: Friend or Foe?

Students' attitudes toward the future have a critical effect on education, yet they are frequently ignored by schools. More than a decade ago, Arthur Stinchcombe did an extensive study of high school students and concluded that the factor which distinguished student rebels from achievers was *not* their backgrounds, but rather their expectations for the future.[2] Benjamin Singer has summarized a good deal of additional research which indicates that the same is true at all age-levels, right down to pre-school children in Head Start programs.[3] If what Singer calls their "Future Focused Role Image" (FFRI) is negative or weak, the students are likely to do poorly and to become trouble-makers and eventually dropouts. On the other hand, students with a strong positive FFRI, regardless of their economic or ethnic backgrounds, tend to do well academically and to treat the school's sanctions on disruptive behavior as meaningful.

In a way, this is just common sense. If the future holds nothing for you, education is just a boring irrelevancy which somebody else tries to do to you. And unless your teachers manage to change your mind about what the future holds, it is highly unlikely that they will manage to teach you anything else.

Thus, future-oriented education should always begin with the child's own perception of her/his personal future. If that conception is weak or negative, it needs to be strengthened before anything else can be done educationally. Two basic approaches are most useful: role-modeling and contagious expectations. Acting out possible adult roles and observing persons with whom the student can identify both provide the student with temporary FFRI's which she/he can try on to see how they fit.[4] Whenever a compatible role is found, the student's own sense of what is possible/desirable is strengthened. The effect is greatly amplified if the adults who know the student clearly indicate that they expect her/him to be able to achieve such a role.[5]

Attitudes about the future include more than just self-image, however. It is possible for students with relatively high self-confidence to view the future bleakly if they believe that society as a whole is set on a disastrous course. This is particularly likely to occur as an unintentional side-effect of a futures course which begins by examining the problems facing society. As the summary in Chapter 4 indicates, these can begin to look pretty formidable. As with the personal self-image, the cures are a *thorough* exploration of positive alternatives and the sincere conviction on the part of the teacher that these alternatives can be reached if we try.

The Adaptive Individual

The degree to which schools shape the personalities of their students is very much an open question. For a long time, the public

The Psychology of the Future

assumption has been that schools have a major impact in a very deterministic way—thus the emphasis on building character, and other code-terms for "teaching" morality, discipline, maturity, etc. A cynic might well argue that the debate between free and traditional schools is simply a debate over which kinds of young people are to be made uncomfortable, those who need freedom or those who need authority. Nevertheless, it still seems reasonable to assume that any highly structured system of rewards and penalties applied for 12 years of childhood and adolescence will have some effect on personality, even if not always the intended effect.

If this is the case, then it is also reasonable to inquire into kinds of personality traits which might be desirable and the types of schooling which might best encourage their development. The definition of "desirable" is, of course, open to wide-ranging philosophical debate. Futurism side-steps this debate somewhat by making the pragmatic assumption that *survival* is highly desirable, and that a basic survival requirement is the psychological ability to cope with rapid change.

A necessary corollary of change is that the basic reference points of society are continually being revised and replaced. This puts a major handicap on those individuals who define their own self-image primarily in terms of their relationships to external institutions. As these external references are stripped away, the outer-directed individual may find her/himself with no sense of identity in the present—a prisoner of nostalgia. A premium is therefore placed on a strong independent self-concept. The autonomous and inner-directed individual has, in effect, an internal "anchor" which provides a core of stability in the midst of turmoil.

Another key attribute is that of a comparatively nonabsolutist belief system, in which a small number of fundamental principles are used to organize a great many, more or less tentative values and beliefs. The advantages are that a "fact" which is found to be false can be discarded without threatening the integrity of the whole belief system, and that a means which serves a valuable end in one context can be supplanted by another which serves the same end better in a different context.[6] A more rigid personality, on the other hand, tends to look for "truth" and "morality" in the dictums of revealed authority. This greatly reduces flexibility, since the questioning or revision of any fact or moral judgment also questions the validity of the authority—and therefore threatens to undermine *all* the beliefs in the system.[7]

An autonomous self-image and a non-absolutist belief system

both tend to reduce the threat to an individual of new ideas or information. The result is a third important attribute: *openness*—the quality of being receptive to many different points of view. To one extent or another, everyone practices avoidance of unpleasant or threatening information, but individuals who attempt to screen out *all* contrary viewpoints deprive themselves of the negative feedback which is essential for continuing adaptation. Those who can be more accepting of others are more likely to be able to grow with the situation.

The same factors which reward openness also reward curiosity and imagination. The advantages of curiosity are obvious, since change, by definition, means a constant flow of new information. The need for imagination goes back to Toffler's solution for future shock: *forewarned forearmed.* The future will be full of surprises, but the individual who delights in a wide-ranging game of "what if?" is unlikely to be startled often by unanticipated events.

The final attribute—an attitude of pragmatic idealism—is perhaps somewhat harder to justify, but is just as important. Idealism is a survival trait for anyone caught in a society facing as many fundamental problems as this one. It is also the source of a basic sense of mission, without which life seems meaningless.[8] But idealism means little unless it has some constructive impact on the world. All too often, those who most fervently want to improve conditions put their energies into expressions of outrage or piety which provide emotional catharsis but accomplish little else. A more pragmatic approach, on the other hand, involves a thorough search for high leverage points in the system and an avoidance of "obvious" solutions; although less dramatic, it is ultimately more satisfying and more honest. It is also only by choosing and acting *effectively* that one can regain a sense of control, the knowledge that one is not merely being swept along by the current, but has some say in the destination.

Each of these attributes is individually important as an objective of future-oriented education. Taken together, they describe what Abraham Maslow termed the "self-actualizing" individual.[9] Maslow and others have done extensive studies on the conditions which foster self-actualization, conditions which constitute an environment "that reacts to experimentation without censoring, effort with appropriate reward, confusion with explanation, anger with understanding, love with love."[10]

Since this constitutes a fair approximation of the goals of progressive education, a substantial body of research exists on the

The Psychology of the Future

establishment of such an environment in the classroom.[11] Although the goals of open education are usually advocated on philosophical grounds, a hard-headed look at the future indicates that these may also be the most desirable goals from a pragmatic, survival point of view.

Teaching the Future

In summary, then, what does future-oriented education mean for the classroom teacher? Ideally, it would mean working with all of the teachers and staff in the school to develop and implement an educational program which:

- Begins with the student's own personal image of the future, working to strengthen it where necessary.

- Relates *all* subject matter to the future needs of the students.

- Apportions space in the curriculum to different subjects according to their relevance to the students' futures, explains the rationale for the curriculum choices to students, and allows the flexibility to accommodate differences in interests, ability, and future plans.

- Presents content in an interdisciplinary manner, emphasizing the underlying similarities of all living and social systems.

- Organizes the learning environment to stimulate creativity, self-motivated learning, and self-discovery.

- Emphasizes skills over knowledge, helping students learn "sciencing" as well as science, forecasting as well as forecasts—in short, thinking as well as facts.

Most teachers, however, will not be fortunate enough to work in a school-wide setting, free from the detailed dictates of legislatures and school boards as to what will be taught. Even with no outside cooperation, elementary teachers who stay with the same class can come quite close to achieving the goals outlined above for the whole school. Subject-matter specialists will necessarily have to be more selective in the future-oriented goals they try to achieve while still meeting their obligations to "cover the subject." And in most high schools, it will be possible to offer a course on the future, either as an elective or as the senior year of social studies or humanities.

Whichever route is taken, the personal rewards for the teacher are high. Even if future studies were not important in itself, it would be an excellent motivational "gimmick." It is not a gimmick, however, but a vitally necessary approach to education, and teachers who commit themselves to it are entitled to enjoy the enthusiasm of their students, as well as a sense of pride in having made a significant contribution to their future well-being.

References

References

Chapter One—Introduction
1. Kahn and Wiener [1967], pp. 64-65.
2. Wofsy, McElroy, and Sze, *Science* [14 February 1975], pp. 535-536.
3. McHale [1972], pp. 1-6.
4. Michael [1968], p. 106; and Toffler [1970], pp. 289-326.
5. McHale [1969], p. 59.
6. Tugwell [1973], pp. vi-xvi.
7. The Commission on Population Growth and the American Future [1972], p. 15.
8. J. C. Parker, *et al.*, "Philosophies and Aims of Education," in Stone and Schneider [1971], pp. 511-513.
9. The estimate is almost certainly too conservative. Richard Stock conducted a survey in 1973-74 in which he identified 571 future studies teachers at the secondary level alone [presentation to the World Future Society Conference on "Teaching Futures," Oct. 5, 1974]. Assuming that he reached 10% of the teachers then involved, and that involvement has doubled in two years, the total for 1975-76 would be more than 11,000.
10. E.g., Toffler [1974], Mead [1970], and Shane, *Phi Delta Kappan* [Vol. 54, January 1973], pp. 326-339.
11. Personal communication from Billy Rojas (assistant to Alvin Toffler), June 1975.
12. Richard Stock [see footnote 9, above].
13. Based on the personal observations of teachers the author has worked with or met at conferences and workshops on future studies. The sample (n = 100?) is decidedly nonrandom; on the other hand, the observations have been unanimous.

Chapter Two—The Alternative Futures Approach
1. Tugwell [1973], pp. vi-xvi.
2. *Ibid.*
3. See McHale [1972] for an excellent source of trends for classroom discussion.
4. Ayres [1969], p. 99.
5. On constrained variables generally, see Ayres [1969], pp. 105-108.
6. Helmer and Rescher, "On the Epistomology of the Inexact Sciences," in Tugwell [1973], pp. 50-74.
7. Ayres [1969], pp. 143-144.
8. *Ibid.*, pp. 143-158.
9. Harman, *et al.* [1970].
10. Kahn and Wiener [1967], p. 6 and pp. 262-264.
11. Ayres [1969], p. 146.

Chapter Three—Systems, Stability, and Change
1. Laszlo [1972].
2. *Ibid.*, pp. 3-20.
3. Meadows, *et al.* [1972], p. 35.
4. Laszlo [1972], p. 41.

FUTURISM AND FUTURE STUDIES

5. *Ibid.*
6. *Ibid.*
7. Cf., Kauffman [1975], p. 8.15.
8. Benjamin Singer, "The Future-Focused Role-Image," in Toffler [1974], p. 21.
9. Platt [1966], pp. 87–107.
10. Jay W. Forrester, "Counterintuitive Behavior of Social Systems," in Tugwell [1973], pp. 198–208.
11. Haveman and Knopf [1970], pp. 226–233.
12. *U.S. News and World Report* [March 3, 1975], pp. 87–89.
13. Ehrlich and Ehrlich [1970], p. 10.
14. Jay W. Forrester, "Counterintuitive Behavior of Social Systems," in Tugwell [1973], pp. 198–208.
15. Forrester [1971], pp. 2–5.
16. Meadows, *et al.* [1972], p. 30.
17. Nobile and Deedy [1972], p. 15.
18. Meadows, *et al.* [1972], p. 19.
19. See, for example: Meadows, *et al.* [1972] and Mesarovic and Pestel [1975].
20. Bell and Mau [1971], pp. 18–29.
21. *Ibid.*, p. 21

Chapter Four—Key Issues
1. Fay Willey, *et al.*, "Who's Going Nuclear?" *Newsweek* [July 7, 1975], p. 27.
2. Scrimshaw, *Technology Review* [December 1974], pp. 13–19.
3. Quigg, *Saturday Review* [January 11, 1975], p. 63.
4. Scrimshaw, *Technology Review* [December 1974], p. 14.
5. International Bank for Reconstruction and Development [1973].
6. *Ibid.*
7. See McHale [1972], p. 95; and Meadows [1972], pp. 69–72.
8. Detwyler [1971], p. 6.
9. *Ibid.*, p. 15
10. Samuelson [1964], pp. 36–55.
11. Hardin, *The North American Review* [Winter 1974], pp. 14–17.
12. Samuelson [1964], p. 466.
13. *Ibid.*, pp. 250–261.
14. Friedman [1974].
15. On advice of Arnold B. Draper, Sandia Corporation, Albuquerque, N.M.
16. For example, see Friedman [1974].
17. S. Porter, quoted in Norman [1974], p. 110, and Toffler [1970], p. 98.
18. Tussing, *Intellect* [February 1975], pp. 303–311; "When You Look Behind the Figures of U.S. Joblessness," *U.S. News and World Report*, February 3, 1975, pp. 61–63; Lindley H. Clark, Jr., "Outlook," *Wall Street Journal*, March 3, 1975, p. 1; and Geoffrey H. Moore, "A Measuring Stick for Employment," *Wall Street Journal*, May 9, 1975, p. 12.
19. Udry [1966], pp. 211–212.
20. Meadows, *et al.* [1972].

References

21. Platt [1966], pp. 108–131.
22. Greenspan, *The Wall Street Journal* [March 19, 1974].
23. Abelson, *Science* [4 July 1975], p. 11.
24. *Ibid.*
25. Burby [1971], pp. 268–294.
26. Maslow, "A Theory of Human Motivation: the Goals of Work," in Best [1973], pp. 27–28.
27. Patterson, *Change* [March 1975], pp. 10–11.
28. *Ibid.*, p. 11.
29. Bell [1973], pp. 425–433.
30. *Ibid.*
31. Commoner [1972], pp. 119–124.
32. Rocks and Runyon [1972], p. 22.
33. Hammond, *Science* [11 July 1975], pp. 128–130.
34. *Newsweek* [January 21, 1974], pp. 79–80.
35. Hubbert, "Energy Resources," in Committee on Resources and Man [1969], pp. 207–218; and Axtmann, *Science* [7 March 1975], pp. 795–803.
36. Gofman [1971].
37. *Time* [February 17, 1975], p. 86.
38. Hammond, [1974], pp. 279–280; and *Newsweek* [February 24, 1975].
39. Commoner [1972], pp. 119–124; and Taylor and Humpstone [1973].
40. *The Futurist* [December 1974]; and Hammond [1974].
41. Vacroux, *Scientific American* [May 1975], p. 32.
42. Miller [1971], pp. 24–53.
43. *Science* [20 December 1974], pp. 1102–1104.
44. *Ibid.*
45. Platt [1966], pp. 3–18.
46. Cohen, *Scientific American* [July 1975], pp. 25–33.

Chapter Five—The Psychology of the Future
1. Toffler [1970], p. 371.
2. Bell and Mau [1971], p. 33.
3. Singer, "The Future-Focused Role-Image," in Toffler [1974], pp. 19–32.
4. *Ibid.*, pp. 21–25.
5. *Ibid.*, p. 24.
6. Russell [1949], pp. 94–101.
7. *Ibid.*
8. Maslow, "A Theory of Human Motivation: the Goals of Work," in Best [1973], p. 26.
9. *Ibid.*, pp. 17–31.
10. Mitchell, "Human Needs and the Changing Goals of Life and Work," in Best [1973], p. 35.
11. Parker, *et al.*, "Philosophies and Aims of Education," in Stone and Schneider [1971], pp. 511–513.

53

Bibliography

Bibliography

A companion to this monograph is *Teaching the Future: A Guide to Future-Oriented Education*, by the same author (Palm Springs, Calif.: ETC Publications, 1976). It is a handbook of classroom activities which can be used in a variety of settings for introducing students to different ways of thinking about the future.

Other useful sources for future-oriented teaching and curriculum planning are listed below.

Abt, Clark C. *Serious Games*. New York: Viking, 1970.

Armstrong, J. Scott. *Long-Range Forecasting: From Crystal Ball to Computer*. New York: Wiley-Interscience, 1978.

Ayres, Robert U. *Technological Forecasting and Long-Range Planning*. New York: McGraw-Hill, 1969.

Bell, Wendell, and James A. Mau, eds. *The Sociology of the Future*. New York: Russell Sage Foundation, 1971.

Best, Fred, ed. *The Future of Work*. Englewood Cliffs, NJ: Prentice-Hall, 1973.

Boulding, Kenneth E. *The Meaning of the Twentieth Century*. New York: Harper and Row, 1964.

Bowman, Jim, et al. *The Far Side of the Future: Social Problems and Educational Reconstruction*. Washington, D.C.: World Future Society, 1978.

Brown, Lester R. *The Twenty-Ninth Day*. New York: W. W. Norton, 1978.

Cornish, Edward. *The Study of the Future*. Washington, D.C.: World Future Society, 1977.

———, ed. *The Future: A Guide to Information Sources*. Washington, D.C.: World Future Society, 1979.

David, E. E., et al. *The Man-Made World*. New York: McGraw-Hill, 1971. (A systems-oriented engineering text for high school.)

Davis, W. Jackson. *The Seventh Year: Industrial Civilization in Transition*. New York: W. W. Norton, 1979.

deJouvenel, Bertrand. *The Art of Conjecture*. New York: Basic Books, 1967.

Detwyler, Thomas R. *Man's Impact on the Environment*. New York: McGraw-Hill, 1971.

Didsbury, Howard F. *The Study of the Future—A Manual for Teachers*. Washington, D.C.: World Future Society, 1979.

———. *The Study of the Future—Study Guide for Students*. Washington, D.C.: World Future Society, 1979.

Drucker, Peter F. *The Age of Discontinuity*. New York: Harper and Row, 1969.

Eckholm, Erik P. *Losing Ground*. New York: W. W. Norton, 1976.

Ehrlich, Paul R. and Anne H., and John P. Holdren. *Ecoscience: Population, Resources, Environment*. San Francisco: W. H. Freeman, 1977.

Ferkiss, Victor C. *The Future of Technological Civilization*. New York: George Braziller, 1974.

———. *Futurology: Promises, Performances, Prospects.* Beverly Hills, Calif. Sage Publications, 1977.

Franks, Betty Barclay, and Mary Kay Howard. *People, Law, and the Futures Perspective.* Washington, D.C.: National Education Association, 1979.

Friedman, Milton. *Capitalism and Freedom.* Chicago: University of Chicago Press, 1962.

Hardin, Garrett. *Exploring New Ethics for Survival.* San Francisco: W. H. Freeman, 1972.

Harman, Willis W. *An Incomplete Guide to the Future.* San Francisco: San Francisco Book Company, 1976.

Heathers, Glen, et al. *Educators Guide for the Future.* Philadelphia: Research for Better Schools, 1977.

Helmer, Olaf. *Orienting Education Toward the Future.* Los Angeles: Center for Futures Research, 1977.

Horn, Robert E. *The Guide to Simulations/Games for Education and Training.* Cranford, N.J.: Didactic Systems, 1977.

Kauffman, Draper L. *Teaching the Future.* Palm Springs, Calif.: ETC Publications, 1976.

Laszlo, Ervin. *The Systems View of the World.* New York: George Braziller, 1972.

McHale, John. *World Facts and Trends.* New York: Collier, 1972.

Marien, Michael. *Societal Directions and Alternatives: A Critical Guide to the Literature.* Lafayette, N.Y.: Information for Policy Design, 1976.

Martin, James. *The Wired Society.* Englewood Cliffs, N.J.: Prentice-Hall, 1978.

Meadows, Donella H., et al. *The Limits to Growth.* New York: Universe Books, 1972.

Miller, George, et al. *Plans and the Structure of Behavior.* New York: Holt, Rinehart, and Winston, 1960.

Miller, James G. *Living Systems.* New York: McGraw-Hill, 1978.

Parkman, Ralph. *The Cybernetic Society.* New York: Pergamon Press, 1972.

Platt, John. *The Step to Man.* New York: John Wiley, 1966.

Russell, Bertrand. *Authority and the Individual.* Boston: Beacon Press, 1960. (Orig. pub. 1949.)

Shane, Harold G. *Curriculum Change Toward the 21st Century.* Washington, D.C.: National Education Association, 1977.

Toffler, Alvin. *Future Shock.* New York: Random House, 1970.

———, ed. *The Futurists.* New York: Random House, 1972.

———, ed. *Learning for Tomorrow: The Role of the Future in Education.* New York: Random House, 1974.

———. *The Third Wave.* New York: Morrow, 1980.

Tugwell, Franklin, ed. *Search for Alternatives: Public Policy and the Study of the Future.* Cambridge, Mass.: Winthrop, 1973.

Watt, Kenneth E. F. *The Titanic Effect: Planning for the Unthinkable.* New York: E. P. Dutton, 1974.

LIBRARY OF DAVIDSON COLLEGE

Books on regular loan may be checked out for **two weeks**. Books must be presented at the Circulation Desk in order to be renewed.

A fine is charged after date due.

Special books are subject to special regulations at the discretion of the library staff.